Kingdom Money: Unlocking Biblical Secrets to Financial Success

1. Put God First...9

2. Avoid Debt...21

3. Be Content and Avoid Greed...35

4. Save for the Future...48

5. Work Diligently...62

6. Help Those in Need...75

7. Be Honest in Financial Dealings...88

8. Don't Place Trust in Wealth...101

9. Budget Wisely...115

10. Invest Wisely...128

Discover the Path to Financial Freedom with Kingdom Money: Unlocking Biblical Secrets to Financial Success

Are you ready to transform your finances and honor God in every financial decision? Kingdom Money unveils the timeless wisdom of Scripture, offering practical guidance to align your financial life with God's will.

This book breaks down essential biblical principles into 10 actionable chapters, covering everything from putting God first to managing wealth with integrity. Whether you're struggling with debt, seeking to build wealth, or simply wanting to handle your money God's way, this book is your roadmap.

Learn how to:

• Prioritize God in your finances by giving generously and trusting His provision.

• Break free from debt and live within your means.

• Cultivate contentment and avoid the trap of greed.

- Plan for the future with saving and wise investing.

- Give back to those in need and reflect God's heart of generosity.

Each chapter is enriched with biblical references, practical tips, and real-world applications, making it easy to put these principles into practice.

Don't settle for worldly advice when God's Word offers a plan for lasting financial peace and success. Kingdom Money empowers you to become a faithful steward, build wealth wisely, and leave a legacy of generosity.

Take the first step toward financial freedom today. Order your copy of Kingdom Money: Unlocking Biblical Secrets to Financial Success and start living in alignment with God's financial plan for your life!

About Scott Perdue

Scott Perdue is a dynamic entrepreneur, author, and community leader with a life rooted in faith, family, and service. A devoted Christian, Scott has been married for over 20 years and is the proud father of four children—two girls and two boys. His passion for personal development and spiritual growth is reflected in his prolific writing career, having authored over 80 books, most of which focus on self-help and Christian themes. His books have touched the lives of countless readers seeking guidance on how to lead a fulfilling, faith-centered life.

For over 15 years, Scott has been a dedicated member of GUTS Church, a place he fondly refers to as "It Takes GUTS to Serve the Lord." His service to the church and community extends beyond attendance; he spent six years as a representative for the GUTS Food Bank, where he managed the movement of wholesale goods to help those in need. Scott also led a successful Maximized Manhood study group based on Edwin Cole's teachings, further exemplifying his commitment to fostering spiritual growth among men.

An accomplished entrepreneur, Scott has started and operated over 30 businesses, ranging from pest control to contracting. He is the founder of Universal Bug Man, a pest control service where Scott earned a reputation as a "pest control superhero." His entrepreneurial ventures include Tulsa Furniture Wholesale, Tulsa Auction Spot, and Builderhaus Unlimited, among others. Scott's business acumen extends to the health and wellness industry, where his company HCG Medical helped over 20,000 clients lose weight, generating over $6.5 million in sales in its best year.

Scott Perdue is a man of many talents, driven by his faith and dedication to serving others through his varied enterprises and writing.

Scott Perdue Books (on Amazon)

Christian Books by Scott Perdue:

Biblical Entrepreneur Leadership: Amplified Leverage Business Skills Book & Workbook

Biblical Men's Leadership Skills: Becoming an Amplified Christian Superstar Book & Workbook

Unleashing Biblical Manhood: Taking Ground Like a Warrior Book & Workbook

Promised Land Leadership: Leading an Army Like Joshua

Wilderness Wisdom of Moses: Timeless Life-Changing Leadership Lessons

Rules of Christianity According to Paul Book & Workbook

Provisional Miracles of Jesus: Provision through Supernatural Means Book & Workbook

The King's Highway: Lean into Jesus for Accelerated Success

Walk in the Works of the Lord: An Amplified Passion Understanding

God's River: Getting into the Kingdom Family Flow

Forgiven & Unoffendable: The Power of Walking Righteously

God is Real: Knowing the Spirit - A Journey Through Faith, Miracles, and Divine Presence

Living on Purpose: A Comprehensive Guide to a Meaningful and Fulfilling Life

Praying for Others: Unlocking your God-Given Authority to Change Lives

Speaking in Tongues: Snippets of Life Improvement Code

Be Fruitful and Multiply: A Biblical Guide to Family Planning and Takes

Biblical Map of the Garden of Eden: Where does this Mysterious Garden Exist?

Methuselah: The Biblical Legacy of Noah's Grandfather

Love's Crossroads: The Rewards of Suffering for Love

Features of a Great Christian Camp: A Priority Spiritual Foundation

Daily Mercy: A Journey Through God's Grace Every Morning

Self Help Books by Scott Perdue:

You Are the Masterpiece: Center of the Universe Life Experience

Legacy Blueprint: How to Build a Generational Legacy

Accomplishing Greatness: 10 Legendary Skill Sets of Self-Made Millionaires

Beginners Guide to Investing in the Future: Gain Wealth from Cutting Edge Sectors

Motivation for Creation: Unlocking the Spark Within

10 Step Productivity Plan: A Guide to Increasing Life's Results

Mindset of Productivity: A Defined Focused Journey

Mindful Love: Embracing Self Love Through Mindfulness and Compassion

The Ultimate Guide to Winning Friends and Influencing People: Master Communication

The Human Connection: Unlocking the Secrets to Understanding and Relating to Others

Mind Switch: Are you Over-Thinking Negative Thoughts?

Mastering Self-Control: Unleashing the Power of Discipline for Success in Every Aspect of Life

Unlocking Secrets to Weight Loss: A Comprehensive Guide to Science, Nutrition, and Wellness

Effective Diet Supplements for Weight Loss

The Body Detox Blueprint: 10 Essential Steps to Cleanse, Heal, and Revitalize Your Body

Secret 1000 Calorie Cryogenic Diet

Learn to Enjoy Reading: Your Ultimate Guide to Loving Books

The Ultimate Blueprint to Comedy: Your Guide to Mastering Humor and Making People Laugh

Decluttering Your Home: Take Control of Your Space, One Step at a Time

Real Estate Needs Observation: Hot to Bring Light to Entropy & Chaos

Business Books by Scott Perdue:

Legendary Business Skills: How to Think like an Entrepreneur

Seal the Deal: Mastering Sales Objections to Close Every Sale

10 Step Marketing Launch: Ultimate Guide for a Business Advertising Start Up

Email Marketing Success: 10 Ways to Master Business Email Advertising Strategy

Controlled Decent: How to Close a Business

How to Start a Business Networking Group: Learn to Organize and Motivate Business Leaders

Negotiate Like an Auctioneer: Mastering the Art of Persuasion and Control

Auction House Blueprint: How to Win Bids and Host a Successful Auction

How to Run an Antique Shop: Restoring Antique Relics to Modern Living

Secondhand Success: A Complete Guide to Running a Profitable Used Furniture Store

The Thrift Store Playbook: How to Build, Manage, and Thrive in the Resale Business

How to Start an RV Park: Your Roadmap to Success

Turn Rapids to Revenue: How to Run a Profitable River Float Business

Science Books by Scott Perdue:

Creation of Your Galactic Record: Big Bang, DNA, Zodiac, Creation of the Universe. Boom!

Quantum Cosmos: The Wave Function of the Universe

An Astronauts Heavenly Perspective: Planet, Society and Economy

Earth is the Seed of Life: A Geometric Flower of Life

Infinite Plants in Every Seed

Dodecahedron Earth: Exploring the Geometric Key to the Flower of Life

Pangaea Cracked Open: A Pre-Flood World without Oceans

Ancient Cathedral Architecture: A Language Of Semantics Lost in Time

Power Independence: DIY Guide to Building Off-Grid Energy Systems

Harvesting Heaven: The Ultimate Guide to DIY Rainwater Collection Systems

Farming Tactics for the Sahara Desert: Ultimate Gardening Guide for Arid Takes

Easy to Find Herbal Remedies

How to Build Free Energy Lighting: 10 Effective Easy to Build Free Energy Lights

Dynamic Forces: Exploring the Undeniable Power of Movement

Creative Books by Scott Perdue:

Zeppelin Airship Enterprise: The Future of Flight and Travel Reimagined

Ancient Plasma Energy Weapons Revealed: The Lost Technology of Energy Weapons

Echoes of Camelot: Unveiling the Secrets and Legends of the Knights

Secret Treasures of Rome Revealed: Explore the Ancient Architecture of Rome

Giants, Nephilim, and the Legacy of Humanity: From Ancient Myths to Modern Mysteries

Prophecy of the Seven Suns: Exploring Parhelia in Biblical Prophecy

Epic Scavenger Hunt of Machu Picchu

Adventures of Buying an Island: Edge of Your Seat Suspense Thriller Adventure

My Neighbor is an Inventor: A Journey into Wilson's World of Innovation

Adventures of the Zoo Janitor: Growing Responsibility By Excellence

Exile's Genesis: Chronicles of the New Frontier

Relics of Oklahoma: Route 66 Treasure Hunt

The Oklahoma Waterfall Hunt

Put God First

Managing finances in alignment with God's Word is more than a practical endeavor—it's an act of faith, trust, and worship. Unlock Biblical Secrets to Financial Success reveals how biblical principles can transform your relationship with money, enabling you to honor God, achieve financial stability, and live a life of generosity and peace. The Bible teaches that by putting God first, practicing wise stewardship, and living with an open hand, we can unlock divine blessings and financial peace.

Put God First: Honor the Lord with Your Wealth

At the heart of biblical financial success is the principle of putting God first.

Proverbs 3:9-10 (AMP) instructs: "Honor the Lord with your wealth and with the first fruits of all your crops (income); then your barns will be abundantly filled, and your vats will overflow with new wine."

Honoring God with our wealth means recognizing that all we have comes from Him. When we give the first portion of our income—the tithe—we acknowledge His sovereignty over our resources. Tithing isn't just about money; it's about faith. It demonstrates our trust in God's provision, even when giving may feel like a sacrifice.

The Purpose and Power of Tithing

The tithe, defined as 10% of one's income, was established in the Old

Testament as a way for God's people to support the work of the temple and the Levites (Numbers 18:21). In Malachi 3:10 (AMP), God offers a profound promise tied to tithing: "Bring all the tithes (the tenth) into the storehouse, so that there may be food in My house, and test Me now in this," says the Lord of hosts, "if I will not open for you the windows of heaven and pour out for you [so great] a blessing until there is no more room to receive it."

Tithing unlocks blessings, not just materially but spiritually. It fosters humility, gratitude, and dependence on God. It also aligns our hearts with God's purposes, reminding us that our resources are tools for His kingdom work.

Savings: Practicing Biblical Stewardship

The Bible also emphasizes the importance of saving and planning for the future. Proverbs 21:20 (AMP) states: "There is precious treasure and oil in the dwelling of the wise [who prepare for the future], but a short-sighted and foolish man swallows it up and wastes it."

Saving is a form of stewardship that reflects wisdom and foresight. It's not about hoarding wealth, which the Bible warns against (Luke 12:15-21), but about preparing for future needs and responsibilities.

Consider the example of Joseph in Genesis 41. When Pharaoh dreamed of a coming famine, Joseph advised storing up grain during the years of plenty to provide for the years of lack. This strategy not only saved Egypt but also positioned Joseph as a wise and trusted leader.

Savings also allow us to handle unexpected expenses without falling into debt. Proverbs 22:7 (AMP) warns: "The rich rules over the poor, and the borrower is servant to the lender." By living within our means and setting aside a portion of our income, we can avoid the financial bondage of debt and maintain our freedom to give generously.

Generosity: Reflecting God's Heart

Generosity is a cornerstone of kingdom finances. Proverbs 19:17 (AMP) declares: "He who is gracious and lends a hand to the poor lends to the

Lord, and the Lord will repay him for his good deed."

When we give to others, especially those in need, we reflect God's character. God is a generous giver, providing for us abundantly (James 1:17). As His followers, we are called to mirror that generosity, trusting that He will supply all our needs (Philippians 4:19).

Generosity is not limited to material wealth; it also includes our time, talents, and encouragement. Luke 6:38 (AMP) promises: "Give, and it will be given to you. They will pour into your lap a good measure—pressed down, shaken together, and running over [with no space left for more]. For with the standard of measurement you use [when you do good to others], it will be measured to you in return."

The Biblical Path to Wealth

The Bible offers a clear path to financial success rooted in faith, diligence, and integrity. Consider these key principles:

1. Diligent Work

Hard work is essential to building wealth. Proverbs 13:4 (AMP) states: "The soul (appetite) of the lazy person craves and gets nothing [for lethargy overcomes ambition], but the soul (appetite) of the diligent who works willingly is rich and abundantly supplied."

God blesses effort and initiative, but wealth gained through laziness or dishonesty will not last (Proverbs 21:5).

2. Honesty in Financial Dealings

Integrity is vital in all financial matters. Proverbs 11:1 (AMP) warns: "A false balance and dishonest business practices are extremely offensive to the Lord, but an accurate scale is His delight." Honest dealings honor God and build trust with others.

3. Contentment and Gratitude

True wealth is found in contentment. 1 Timothy 6:6-10 (AMP) teaches: "But godliness actually is a source of great gain when accompanied by contentment [that contentment which comes from a sense of inner confidence based on the sufficiency of God]."

Chasing wealth for its own sake leads to ruin, but trusting in God's provision brings peace.

4. Wise Investment

Investing wisely is a biblical principle. Ecclesiastes 11:2 (AMP) advises: "Divide your portion [among seven, or even eight], for you do not know what misfortune may occur on the earth." Diversifying resources and planning for the long term demonstrate prudent stewardship.

5. Trusting God, Not Wealth

Wealth is uncertain, but God's provision is secure. 1 Timothy 6:17 (AMP) reminds us: "As for the rich in this present world, instruct them not to be conceited and arrogant, nor to set their hope on the uncertainty of riches, but on God, who richly and ceaselessly provides us with everything for our enjoyment."

Prioritizing Finances God's Way

To prioritize money kingdom style, follow these steps:

1. Begin with Tithing

Set aside the first 10% of your income for God's work. This act of obedience invites God's blessings and aligns your heart with His purposes.

2. Create a Budget

Use biblical principles to create a budget that reflects your values. Allocate resources for saving, giving, and necessary expenses.

3. Pay Off Debt

Work diligently to eliminate debt, freeing yourself from financial bondage. Avoid taking on new debt by living within your means.

4. Save and Invest Wisely

Set aside a portion of your income for future needs. Invest in opportunities that align with biblical values and principles.

5. Be Generous
Look for opportunities to bless others. Whether through financial gifts, acts of service, or encouragement, generosity reflects God's love and opens the door for blessings.

6. Trust God in Every Season
Financial success requires faith. Trust God to provide for your needs, even when the path is unclear. Surrendering control allows Him to work in your finances.

A Life of Generosity and Peace

By embracing the stewardship principles outlined in Scripture, you can transform your finances into a tool for God's kingdom. Financial peace is not about accumulating wealth but about using your resources to honor

God, bless others, and fulfill your calling.

Kingdom money management is not just a strategy; it's a lifestyle. As you put God first, save wisely, and give generously, you will experience the joy and freedom that come from living in alignment with His Word. God's promises are sure: as you honor Him with your wealth, He will bless you abundantly, equipping you to live a life of generosity and purpose.

Avoid Debt

Managing money from a biblical perspective requires more than just financial knowledge—it demands faith, discipline, and a commitment to living in alignment with God's principles. The Bible provides timeless wisdom on financial stewardship, offering guidance to avoid debt, save wisely, give generously, and prioritize money in a way that honors God. By understanding and applying these principles, believers can unlock biblical secrets to financial success, find freedom from financial stress, and live a life of generosity and peace.

One of the most critical lessons the Bible teaches about money is the danger of debt. Proverbs 22:7 (AMP) states: "The rich rules over the poor, and the borrower is servant to the lender." This verse paints a vivid picture of the enslavement caused by debt and serves as a call to live within our means. Avoiding debt is not just practical advice; it is a spiritual principle that reflects trust in God's provision and a commitment to financial freedom.

Understanding the Burden of Debt

Debt creates a unique form of bondage. It places individuals under obligation to lenders, limiting their financial freedom and ability to serve God fully. While not inherently sinful, debt can hinder spiritual growth and financial stability when mismanaged. The emotional toll of debt—stress, anxiety, and strained relationships—further illustrates its dangers.

The Bible does not forbid borrowing but warns of its consequences. Romans 13:8 (AMP) says: "Owe nothing to anyone except to love and seek the best for one another." This verse encourages believers to focus on their obligations to love and serve others rather than being weighed down by financial burdens.

Avoiding Debt: A Biblical Approach
1. Live Within Your Means
One of the most effective ways to avoid debt is by living within your means. This requires discipline, contentment, and careful budgeting. Philippians 4:11-12 (AMP) teaches: "I have learned to be content [and self-sufficient through Christ, satisfied to the point where I am not disturbed or uneasy] regardless of my

circumstances." Contentment enables believers to resist the temptation to overspend or accumulate unnecessary possessions.

Creating a budget is a practical way to ensure that spending aligns with income. Proverbs 27:23-24 (AMP) advises: "Be diligent to know the condition of your flocks, and pay attention to your herds; for riches are not forever." Monitoring finances and prioritizing essentials helps prevent debt and ensures financial stability.

2. Practice Delayed Gratification

In a culture that promotes instant gratification, practicing patience is essential. Hebrews 12:11 (AMP) reminds us: "For the time being, no discipline brings joy, but seems sad and painful; yet to those who have been trained by it, afterward it yields the peaceful fruit of righteousness."

Waiting to purchase non-essential items until you can afford them demonstrates wisdom and discipline, reducing reliance on credit.

3. Seek God's Wisdom in Financial Decisions

Before making significant financial commitments, seek God's guidance through prayer and Scripture. James 1:5 (AMP) promises: "If any of you lacks wisdom [to guide him through a decision or circumstance], he is to ask of [our benevolent] God, who gives to everyone generously and without rebuke or blame." Trusting God's timing and direction can help avoid impulsive decisions that lead to debt.

Overcoming Debt

For those already in debt, the Bible offers hope and practical steps to regain financial freedom.

1. Acknowledge the Problem

The first step to overcoming debt is acknowledging its existence and committing to change. Proverbs 28:13 (AMP) states: "He who conceals his transgressions will not prosper, but whoever confesses and turns away [from his sins] will find compassion and mercy." Honesty about financial struggles allows believers to seek help and begin the journey toward freedom.

2. Develop a Repayment Plan

Proverbs 21:5 (AMP) teaches: "The plans of the diligent lead surely to abundance and advantage, but everyone who acts in haste comes surely to poverty." A well-structured repayment plan prioritizes paying off high-interest debts while avoiding new borrowing. This disciplined approach accelerates progress toward financial freedom.

3. Trust in God's Provision
Overcoming debt requires faith in God's ability to provide. Philippians 4:19 (AMP) assures: "And my God will liberally supply (fill until full) your every need according to His riches in glory in Christ Jesus." By trusting in God and relying on His wisdom, believers can navigate financial challenges with confidence and hope.

The Role of Tithing in Financial Freedom

Tithing is a cornerstone of biblical financial principles. Proverbs 3:9-10 (AMP) instructs: "Honor the Lord with your wealth and with the first fruits of all your crops (income); then your barns will be abundantly filled, and your vats will overflow with new wine." Giving the first portion of income to God demonstrates trust in His provision and prioritizes His kingdom over personal desires.

Tithing also aligns the heart with God's purposes. Matthew 6:21 (AMP) states: "For where your treasure is, there your heart will be also." By dedicating a portion of income to God, believers cultivate a spirit of generosity and trust, opening the door for His blessings.

The Importance of Saving

The Bible encourages saving as a form of stewardship and preparation. Proverbs 21:20 (AMP) states: "There is precious treasure and oil in the dwelling of the wise [who prepare for the future], but a short-sighted and foolish man swallows it up and wastes it." Saving allows believers to handle unexpected expenses, avoid debt, and support long-term goals.

Saving is not about hoarding wealth but about being prepared to meet needs and bless others. Joseph's story in Genesis 41 demonstrates the value of saving. By storing grain during years of abundance, Joseph ensured provision for Egypt during a seven-year famine. This principle underscores the importance of planning and foresight in financial stewardship.

Generosity: The Heart of Kingdom Finances

Generosity is a hallmark of biblical financial success. Proverbs 19:17 (AMP) declares: "He who is gracious and lends a hand to the poor lends to the Lord, and the Lord will repay him for his good deed." Giving reflects God's character and allows believers to participate in His work.

Generosity also brings spiritual and practical benefits. Luke 6:38 (AMP) promises: "Give, and it will be given to you. They will pour into your lap a good measure—pressed down, shaken together, and running over [with no space left for more]." A generous spirit unlocks blessings and fosters a sense of community and purpose.

The Biblical Path to Wealth

Biblical wealth is not about accumulating riches but about using resources to honor God and bless others. Key principles for building wealth God's way include:

1. Work Diligently

Proverbs 10:4 (AMP) states: "Poor is he who works with a negligent and idle hand, but the hand of the diligent makes him rich." Hard work and perseverance are essential to financial success.

2. Invest Wisely

Ecclesiastes 11:2 (AMP) advises: "Divide your portion [among seven, or even eight], for you do not know what misfortune may occur on the earth." Diversifying resources and making prudent investments demonstrate stewardship and foresight.

3. Trust in God, Not Wealth

1 Timothy 6:17 (AMP) warns: "As for the rich in this present world, instruct them not to be conceited and arrogant, nor to set their hope on the uncertainty of riches, but on God, who richly and ceaselessly provides us with everything for our enjoyment." Placing trust in God rather than material possessions ensures lasting peace and security.

Prioritizing Finances God's Way

To prioritize money kingdom style, believers must align their financial practices with biblical principles. This involves:
1. Tithing Faithfully
Give the first portion of income to God, trusting Him to provide for all needs.
2. Saving Wisely

Set aside resources for future needs and opportunities to bless others.

3. Avoiding Debt

Live within your means, practice contentment, and avoid unnecessary borrowing.

4. Being Generous

Look for ways to share resources and reflect God's love through giving.

5. Seeking God's Guidance

Pray for wisdom and discernment in all financial decisions.

By following these principles, believers can unlock the secrets to financial success, experience the freedom of debt-free living, and enjoy the blessings of generosity and peace. Kingdom finances are not about wealth accumulation but about faithful stewardship, trusting God, and using resources to advance His purposes. In doing so, we reflect His glory and fulfill our calling as His stewards.

Be Content and Avoid Greed

Managing money from a kingdom perspective begins with aligning our hearts and habits with God's Word. The Bible offers profound guidance on how to prioritize finances in a way that honors God, promotes peace, and fosters generosity. Among its teachings, one principle stands out: the importance of contentment and freedom from greed. Hebrews 13:5 (AMP) exhorts, "Let your character [your moral essence, your inner nature] be free from the love of money [shun greed—be financially ethical], being content with what you have; for He has said, 'I will never [under any circumstances] desert you [nor give you up nor leave you without support].'" This passage underscores the necessity of trusting God for provision, cultivating contentment, and avoiding the trap of materialism.

The Danger of Greed

Greed is a subtle yet powerful force that can lead to financial ruin and spiritual emptiness. Rooted in the desire for more, greed places wealth and possessions above God, disrupting our priorities and diminishing our peace. Jesus warns in Luke 12:15 (AMP): "Be on your guard against every form of greed; for not even when one has an overflowing abundance does his life consist of, nor is it derived from his possessions."

The love of money can enslave the heart, distracting believers from their true purpose. 1 Timothy 6:10 (AMP) cautions, "For the love of money is a root of all sorts of evil, and some by longing for it have wandered away from the faith and pierced themselves through and through with many sorrows." When greed takes hold, it breeds discontentment, fuels impulsive decisions, and leads to financial stress.

The Gift of Contentment

Contentment is the antidote to greed and the foundation of financial peace. It is not complacency but a deep trust in God's provision and sufficiency. Philippians 4:11-13 (AMP) illustrates this beautifully through Paul's testimony: "Not that I speak from [any personal] need, for I have learned to be content [and self-sufficient through Christ, satisfied to the point where I am not disturbed or uneasy] regardless of my circumstances. I know how to get along and live humbly [in difficult times], and I also know how to enjoy abundance and live in prosperity. In any and every circumstance, I have learned the secret [of facing life]—whether well-fed or going hungry, whether having an abundance or being in need. I can do all things [which He has called me to do] through Him who strengthens and empowers me."

Paul's words reveal that contentment is learned through faith and reliance on God, not dependent on external circumstances. It allows believers to resist the constant pull of consumerism and focus on what truly matters—glorifying God and serving others.

Prioritizing Finances Through Contentment

1. Trust in God's Provision

Contentment flows from trusting God to meet our needs. Matthew 6:31-33 (AMP) reminds us: "Therefore do not worry or be anxious, perpetually uneasy or distracted, saying, 'What are we going to eat?' or 'What are we going to drink?' or 'What are we going to wear?' For the [pagan] Gentiles eagerly seek all these things; [but do not worry,] for your heavenly Father knows that you need them. But first and most importantly seek (aim at, strive after) His kingdom and His righteousness [His way of doing and being right—the attitude and character of God], and all these things will be given to you also."

Placing our trust in God frees us from fear and anxiety about financial matters, enabling us to focus on His will and purposes.

2. Practice Gratitude

Gratitude fosters contentment by shifting our focus from what we lack to what we have. 1 Thessalonians 5:18 (AMP) encourages: "In every situation [no matter what the circumstances] be thankful and continually give thanks to God; for this is the will of God for you in Christ Jesus." A thankful heart recognizes God's blessings, big and small, and cultivates satisfaction in His provision.

3. Live Simply

Simplicity is a practical expression of contentment. By living within our means and resisting the urge to accumulate unnecessary possessions, we create space for financial peace and generosity. Proverbs 15:16 (AMP) advises: "Better is a little with the [reverent, worshipful] fear of the Lord than great treasure and trouble with it."

Tithes: Putting God First

A critical step in prioritizing money kingdom style is honoring God with the first portion of our income. Proverbs 3:9-10 (AMP) teaches: "Honor the Lord with your wealth and with the first fruits of all your crops (income); then your barns will be abundantly filled, and your vats will overflow with new wine."

Tithing is an act of worship and trust. It acknowledges that all we have belongs to God and expresses faith in His provision. By giving the first 10% of our income to God, we realign our priorities, placing Him above material concerns. Malachi 3:10 (AMP) reinforces this principle: "Bring all the tithes (the tenth) into the storehouse, so that there may be food in My house, and test Me now in this," says the Lord of hosts, "if I will not open for you the windows of heaven and pour out for you [so great] a blessing until there is no more room to receive it."

Tithing also cultivates a generous spirit, freeing us from greed and fostering a deeper relationship with God.

Savings: A Biblical Strategy for Stewardship

Saving is a practical way to exercise wisdom and stewardship. Proverbs 21:20 (AMP) highlights the importance of preparation: "There is precious treasure and oil in the dwelling of the wise [who prepare for the future], but a short-sighted and foolish man swallows it up and wastes it."

Saving enables believers to handle unexpected expenses, avoid debt, and prepare for future needs. It is not about hoarding wealth but about exercising prudence and planning for God-honoring purposes.

The story of Joseph in Genesis 41 illustrates the value of saving. By storing grain during seven years of abundance, Joseph ensured provision for Egypt during a seven-year famine. This principle underscores the importance of foresight and discipline in financial management.

Generosity: The Heart of Kingdom Finances

Generosity is both a privilege and a responsibility for believers. Acts 20:35 (AMP) declares: "It is more blessed [and brings greater joy] to give than to receive." By sharing our resources, we reflect God's love and participate in His work.

Proverbs 11:25 (AMP) adds: "The generous man [is a source of blessing and] shall be prosperous and enriched, and he who waters will himself be watered [reaping the generosity he has sown]." Generosity brings spiritual and practical rewards, fostering a sense of purpose and community.

Giving also breaks the power of greed and cultivates a spirit of contentment.

It reminds us that our resources are entrusted to us by God for His glory and the benefit of others.

The Biblical Path to Wealth

Biblical wealth is not about amassing riches but about faithful stewardship and advancing God's kingdom. Key principles include:

1. Work Diligently

Proverbs 10:4 (AMP) teaches: "Poor is he who works with a negligent and idle hand, but the hand of the diligent makes him rich." Hard work and perseverance are essential for financial success.

2. Invest Wisely

Ecclesiastes 11:2 (AMP) advises: "Divide your portion [among seven, or even eight], for you do not know what misfortune may occur on the earth."

Diversifying resources and making prudent investments reflect wisdom and stewardship.

3. Trust in God, Not Wealth

1 Timothy 6:17 (AMP) warns: "As for the rich in this present world, instruct them not to be conceited and arrogant, nor to set their hope on the uncertainty of riches, but on God, who richly and ceaselessly provides us with everything for our enjoyment." True security comes from trusting God, not material possessions.

Living in Financial Freedom

By prioritizing money God's way—cultivating contentment, avoiding greed, tithing faithfully, saving wisely, and practicing generosity—believers can experience financial freedom and peace. These principles honor God, reduce financial stress, and enable us to live generously and joyfully.

Ultimately, kingdom finances are about aligning our hearts and habits with God's purposes, trusting Him to provide, and using our resources to reflect His love and advance His kingdom. As we follow His Word and rely on His guidance, we unlock the secrets to true financial success and lasting peace.

Save for the Future

The Bible is a timeless guide for living a life of purpose and peace, including managing finances wisely. Scripture emphasizes the importance of planning, saving, and stewarding resources in ways that honor God and support future stability. In Proverbs 21:20 (AMP), we find this wisdom: "There is precious treasure and oil in the dwelling of the wise [who prepare for the future], but a short-sighted and foolish man swallows it up and wastes it." This verse captures the essence of saving: it reflects wisdom and foresight, enabling us to prepare for future needs while avoiding the pitfalls of impulsive or careless financial decisions.

Saving is not a selfish pursuit but a God-honoring principle that allows us to provide for our families, give generously, and navigate life's uncertainties with peace of mind. By embracing the biblical call to save for the future, we align our financial priorities with kingdom values and unlock the path to true financial success.

The Wisdom of Saving for the Future

Saving demonstrates prudence and responsibility, traits consistently praised in Scripture. From the example of Joseph in Egypt to the teachings of Jesus, the Bible highlights the importance of preparing for what lies ahead.

1. Joseph's Example of Strategic Saving

In Genesis 41, Joseph's interpretation of Pharaoh's dreams led to a nation-wide strategy of saving during seven years of abundance to prepare for seven years of famine. Genesis 41:48-49 (AMP) describes the plan: "During the seven years of plenty the land produced abundantly. And [Joseph] gathered all the surplus food of the seven good years in the land of Egypt and stored enormous quantities of food in the cities."

This example teaches that saving is not about hoarding but about planning wisely to ensure provision during times of scarcity. It also shows how saving enables us to help others in times of need.

2. The Ant as a Model of Diligence
Proverbs 6:6-8 (AMP) points to the ant as a model of foresight and hard work: "Go to the ant, O lazy one; observe her

ways and be wise, which, having no chief, overseer, or ruler, she prepares her food in the summer and brings in her provisions [of food for the winter] in the harvest." This lesson underscores the importance of preparing during times of plenty to ensure stability during times of need.

The Purpose of Saving

Saving is about stewardship, not selfishness. It reflects an understanding that all we have belongs to God and must be managed according to His principles. Here are three biblical purposes for saving:
1. To Provide for Our Families
The Bible emphasizes the responsibility to care for our loved ones. 1 Timothy 5:8 (AMP) states: "If anyone fails to provide for his own, and especially for

those of his own family, he has denied the faith and is worse than an unbeliever." Saving ensures that we can meet the needs of our families, both now and in the future.

2. To Be Generous in Times of Need

By saving wisely, we position ourselves to respond to opportunities for generosity. Proverbs 3:27 (AMP) encourages: "Do not withhold good from those to whom it is due [its rightful recipients], when it is in your power to do it." A well-planned financial life allows us to give freely and joyfully when God calls us to meet the needs of others.

3. To Avoid the Bondage of Debt

Saving helps us avoid unnecessary debt, which the Bible warns against in Proverbs 22:7 (AMP): "The rich rules over the poor, and the borrower is servant to the lender." By setting aside resources, we can cover emergencies and future expenses without falling into the trap of financial slavery.

Practical Steps to Save for the Future

Saving may seem daunting, especially when resources are limited. However, biblical principles offer practical guidance for building a habit of saving:

1. Create a Budget

A budget is a tool for aligning your spending with your priorities. Luke 14:28 (AMP) highlights the importance of planning: "For which one of you, when he wants to build a tower, does not first sit down and calculate the cost [to see if he has enough to finish it]?" Tracking your income and expenses helps identify areas where you can reduce spending and allocate funds toward savings.

2. Start Small and Be Consistent
Even small amounts can grow over time. Proverbs 13:11 (AMP) advises: "Wealth obtained by fraud dwindles, but he who gathers gradually by [honest] labor will increase [his riches]." Consistent saving, no matter how modest, builds discipline and creates a foundation for financial stability.

3. Set Clear Goals
Saving is more effective when tied to specific goals, such as an emergency fund, retirement, or future investments. Habakkuk 2:2 (AMP) says: "Write the vision and engrave it plainly on [clay] tablets so that the one who reads it will run." Clear goals provide motivation and direction for your saving efforts.

4. Avoid Impulse Spending

Proverbs 21:5 (AMP) warns: "The plans of the diligent lead surely to abundance and advantage, but everyone who acts in haste comes surely to poverty." Saving requires self-control and intentionality, resisting the temptation to spend impulsively.

5. Seek God's Guidance

Proverbs 3:5-6 (AMP) reminds us: "Trust in and rely confidently on the Lord with all your heart, and do not rely on your own insight or understanding. In all your ways know and acknowledge and recognize Him, and He will make your paths straight and smooth [removing obstacles that block your way]." Prayer and discernment are essential for managing finances in alignment with God's will.

The Role of Generosity in Financial Stewardship

Saving and generosity are not opposing principles but complementary aspects of biblical stewardship. As we save for the future, we also cultivate a spirit of generosity, recognizing that our resources are entrusted to us by God for His purposes.

1. Generosity Reflects God's Character
God is the ultimate giver, as John 3:16 (AMP) reminds us: "For God so [greatly] loved and dearly prized the world, that He [even] gave His [One and] only begotten Son." By giving to others, we mirror His love and compassion.

2. Generosity Blesses the Giver
Proverbs 11:25 (AMP) states: "The generous man [is a source of blessing and] shall be prosperous and enriched,

and he who waters will himself be watered [reaping the generosity he has sown]." Generosity brings joy, fulfillment, and blessings that transcend material wealth.

3. Generosity Fosters Contentment

Giving shifts our focus from what we lack to what we can share, cultivating gratitude and contentment. Acts 20:35 (AMP) reminds us: "It is more blessed [and brings greater joy] to give than to receive."

Balancing Saving and Giving

The key to balancing saving and giving is seeking God's wisdom and aligning our financial decisions with His priorities. Here are three principles for maintaining this balance:

1. Prioritize Tithing

Tithing—the act of giving the first 10% of our income to God—is a foundational principle of biblical stewardship. Proverbs 3:9-10 (AMP) teaches: "Honor the Lord with your wealth and with the first fruits of all your crops (income); then your barns will be abundantly filled, and your vats will overflow with new wine." By putting God first, we acknowledge His sovereignty and trust Him to meet our needs.

2. Save with Generosity in Mind

Saving is not about accumulating wealth for selfish purposes but about preparing to meet future needs and support others. As we save, we remain open to God's leading, ready to share our resources when opportunities arise.

3. Live Simply and Give Freely

A simple lifestyle creates margin for saving and giving. 1 Timothy 6:6-8 (AMP) reminds us: "But godliness actually is a source of great gain when accompanied by contentment [that contentment which comes from a sense of inner confidence based on the sufficiency of God]. For we have brought nothing into the world, so it is clear that we cannot take anything out of it, either. But if we have food and clothing, with these we will be content."

The Eternal Perspective on Wealth

Ultimately, financial stewardship is not about earthly wealth but eternal impact. Jesus reminds us in Matthew 6:19-21 (AMP): "Do not store up for yourselves treasures on earth, where moth and rust destroy, and where thieves break in and steal. But store up for yourselves treasures in heaven, where neither moth nor rust destroys, and where thieves do not break in and steal; for where your treasure is, there your heart will be also."

By saving wisely, giving generously, and prioritizing God's kingdom, we lay up treasures that will never fade, reflecting His glory and fulfilling His purposes.

Conclusion

Saving for the future is a biblical principle rooted in wisdom, responsibility, and trust in God. It allows us to provide for our families, respond to life's uncertainties, and support God's work through generosity. As we align our financial practices with Scripture—budgeting, saving consistently, avoiding debt, and giving joyfully—we unlock the secrets to financial success and experience the peace and freedom that come from honoring God with our resources.

Through faithful stewardship, we reflect God's character, live out His purposes, and build a legacy that glorifies Him for generations to come.

Work Diligently

The Bible is not silent on financial principles. It provides clear guidance on how to manage resources wisely, work diligently, and plan effectively. Proverbs 21:5 (AMP) states, "The plans of the diligent lead surely to abundance and advantage, but everyone who acts in haste comes surely to poverty." This verse encapsulates the importance of hard work, intentional planning, and persistence in achieving financial success. These principles, rooted in Scripture, form the foundation of managing money kingdom style— honoring God while building a life of peace, generosity, and stability.

In this discussion, we will explore how diligent work, alongside principles like tithing, saving, and generosity, leads to financial growth and positions us to fulfill God's purposes. We will also delve into the biblical path to wealth, emphasizing how to align our financial priorities with God's will.

The Value of Hard Work in God's Kingdom

The Bible repeatedly emphasizes the value of diligence and hard work. While salvation is a gift of grace, success in financial and material matters often requires effort and perseverance. Here are several key lessons from Scripture:

1. Work Is a God-Given Responsibility
Work is not a result of the fall; it was part of God's original design. Genesis 2:15 (AMP) says, "So the Lord God took the man [He had made] and

settled him in the Garden of Eden to cultivate and keep it." This demonstrates that work is honorable and part of God's purpose for humanity.

When we approach work as a form of worship, it takes on greater meaning. Colossians 3:23 (AMP) instructs, "Whatever you do [whatever your task may be], work from the soul [that is, put in your very best effort], as [something done] for the Lord and not for men." Viewing work as service to God motivates us to strive for excellence and integrity.

2. Diligence Brings Prosperity

Proverbs 10:4 (AMP) declares, "Poor is he who works with a negligent and idle hand, but the hand of the diligent makes him rich." This principle reminds us that success often comes not from luck but from consistent effort and commitment.

Whether managing a business, working a job, or pursuing personal goals, diligence involves a steadfast focus on doing things well and finishing what we start. God blesses this kind of dedication because it reflects His own character of faithfulness.

3. Planning Is Part of Diligence

Proverbs 21:5 highlights the connection between diligent planning and financial success. Planning involves setting goals, creating budgets, and making wise decisions about how to use resources. In Luke 14:28-30 (AMP), Jesus underscores the importance of planning: "For which one of you, when he wants to build a tower, does not first sit down and calculate the cost to see if he has enough to finish it?"

A diligent worker doesn't merely labor aimlessly but ensures their efforts are purposeful and aligned with long-term goals.

The Biblical Path to Wealth

The Bible acknowledges wealth as a blessing but warns against pursuing it at the expense of godly values. Proverbs 10:22 (AMP) says, "The blessing of the Lord brings [true] riches, and He adds no sorrow to it [for it comes as a blessing from God]." Wealth gained through honest means and with God's favor enriches lives and enables generosity.

Here are three biblical steps to building wealth the kingdom way:
1. Start with Tithing

Tithing is the act of giving the first 10% of your income back to God. It is a tangible way to honor Him and acknowledge that all we have comes from Him. Malachi 3:10 (AMP) says, "Bring all the tithes (the tenth) into the storehouse, so that there may be food in My house, and test Me now in this," says the Lord of hosts, "if I will not open for you the windows of heaven and pour out for you [so great] a blessing until there is no more room to receive it."

Tithing reflects trust in God's provision and invites His blessings into your finances. It also teaches discipline, contentment, and generosity, which are foundational to financial stewardship.

2. Save for the Future

Proverbs 21:20 (AMP) states, "There is precious treasure and oil in the dwelling of the wise [who prepare for the future], but a short-sighted and foolish man swallows it up and wastes it." Saving is not about hoarding but about preparing for future needs, emergencies, and opportunities.

A diligent saver is like the ant described in Proverbs 6:6-8 (AMP): "Go to the ant, O lazy one; observe her ways and be wise, which, having no chief, overseer, or ruler, she prepares her food in the summer and brings in her provisions [of food for the winter] in the harvest." This model of preparation ensures stability and peace in times of uncertainty.

3. Invest Wisely

Ecclesiastes 11:1-2 (AMP) advises, "Cast your bread on the surface of the waters [be diligently active, make thoughtful decisions], for you will find it after many days. Give a portion to seven, or even [divide it] to eight, for you do not know what misfortune may occur on the earth." This verse encourages diversification and thoughtful investment.

While saving ensures we have resources, investing allows those resources to grow and multiply, creating opportunities for greater impact.

The Role of Generosity in Financial Success

Generosity is a cornerstone of kingdom finances. It reflects God's character, strengthens our faith, and brings joy and fulfillment.

1. Generosity Opens the Door to Blessings

Proverbs 11:25 (AMP) states, "The generous man [is a source of blessing and] shall be prosperous and enriched, and he who waters will himself be watered [reaping the generosity he has sown]." Giving to others not only meets their needs but also invites blessings into our own lives.

2. Generosity Breaks the Power of Greed

Greed is a trap that leads to discontent and spiritual poverty. 1 Timothy 6:10 (AMP) warns, "For the love of money is the root of all sorts of evil, and some by longing for it have wandered away from the faith and pierced themselves through and through with many sorrows." Generosity helps us focus on eternal values rather than earthly possessions.

3. Generosity Multiplies Resources

In Luke 6:38 (AMP), Jesus says, "Give, and it will be given to you. They will pour into your lap a good measure—

pressed down, shaken together, and running over [with no space left for more]." This principle of sowing and reaping applies to finances, time, and talents.

Overcoming Financial Challenges

Even with diligent work and wise stewardship, financial challenges are inevitable. However, the Bible provides guidance for navigating these difficulties:
1. Trust God's Provision
Philippians 4:19 (AMP) assures us, "And my God will liberally supply (fill until full) your every need according to His riches in glory in Christ Jesus." When we face financial struggles, we can trust God to meet our needs in His perfect timing.
2. Avoid the Trap of Debt

Proverbs 22:7 (AMP) warns, "The rich rules over the poor, and the borrower is servant to the lender." Living within our means and avoiding unnecessary debt protects us from financial bondage.

3. Seek Wisdom

James 1:5 (AMP) promises, "If any of you lacks wisdom [to guide him through a decision or circumstance], he is to ask of [our benevolent] God, who gives to everyone generously and without rebuke or blame, and it will be given to him." Prayer and godly counsel provide clarity and direction in difficult times.

Aligning Financial Goals with Kingdom Priorities

Ultimately, financial success in God's kingdom is about more than wealth;

it's about fulfilling His purposes. Matthew 6:33 (AMP) reminds us, "But first and most importantly seek (aim at, strive after) His kingdom and His righteousness [His way of doing and being right—the attitude and character of God], and all these things will be given to you also."

When we prioritize God's kingdom, our finances become a tool for advancing His work, blessing others, and living a life of peace and purpose. By working diligently, saving wisely, and giving generously, we honor God and unlock the true secrets to financial success.

Through faith, discipline, and alignment with biblical principles, we can experience the abundant life Jesus promised, free from financial stress and rich in eternal impact.

Help Those in Need

The Bible is a treasure trove of wisdom for managing finances in a way that honors God and leads to lasting peace and fulfillment. One of the core principles of kingdom-style financial management is generosity—helping those in need. Proverbs 19:17 (AMP) states, "He who is gracious and lends a hand to the poor lends to the Lord, and the Lord will repay him for his good deed." This verse encapsulates the heart of biblical stewardship: treating wealth as a tool to serve others and glorify God.

This summary explores the biblical path to financial success, focusing on tithing, saving, and generosity. It emphasizes how helping the needy is not only a reflection of God's character but also a means to unlock His blessings. By prioritizing finances God's way, we align with His will and cultivate a life marked by generosity, stability, and purpose.

Generosity as a Reflection of God's Heart

God's character is inherently generous. He created a world of abundance and provided for humanity's every need. From the manna that sustained Israel in the wilderness to the ultimate gift of Jesus Christ, God's generosity is boundless.

When we give to others, especially the poor and needy, we mirror this aspect of His nature. Proverbs 19:17 (AMP) assures us that "He who is gracious and lends a hand to the poor lends to the Lord." This verse not only highlights the spiritual significance of generosity but also promises a divine reward for those who practice it.

Helping those in need serves several purposes in God's kingdom:
1. It Demonstrates Love for God and Others
Jesus taught that the greatest commandments are to love God and love our neighbors (Matthew 22:37-39). Acts of generosity fulfill this dual commandment, as they are tangible expressions of love and compassion.
2. It Reflects God's Justice and Mercy
Psalm 82:3 (AMP) commands, "Vindicate the weak and fatherless; do justice and maintain the rights of the afflicted and destitute." Caring for the marginalized is an integral part of living out biblical principles.

3. It Advances God's Kingdom
Generosity creates opportunities for the gospel to be shared. By meeting physical needs, we open hearts to receive spiritual truth.

Tithing: The Foundation of Kingdom Finances

Tithing is the cornerstone of biblical financial stewardship. It involves giving the first 10% of our income back to God as an act of worship and trust. Malachi 3:10 (AMP) declares, "Bring all the tithes (the tenth) into the storehouse, so that there may be food in My house, and test Me now in this," says the Lord of hosts, "if I will not open for you the windows of heaven and pour out for you [so great] a blessing until there is no more room to receive it."

Tithing has both spiritual and practical benefits:

1. It Acknowledges God's Sovereignty

Tithing reminds us that all we have belongs to God. By returning the first portion to Him, we affirm His lordship over our finances.

2. It Invites God's Blessing

The promise in Malachi 3:10 emphasizes that faithful tithing opens the door to divine provision and abundance.

3. It Funds God's Work

Tithes support the church's mission, enabling it to meet spiritual and physical needs within the community.

Saving: Planning for the Future

While generosity is essential, saving is another vital component of biblical financial stewardship. Proverbs 21:20 (AMP) says, "There is precious treasure and oil in the dwelling of the wise [who prepare for the future], but a short-sighted and foolish man swallows it up and wastes it."

Saving demonstrates wisdom, discipline, and foresight. It prepares us for unexpected challenges and positions us to seize opportunities for generosity. Here's how saving aligns with kingdom principles:
1. It Reflects God's Orderliness
God is a God of order and planning. The story of Joseph in Egypt (Genesis 41:47-49) exemplifies this. By storing surplus during years of abundance, Joseph ensured provision during a famine.
2. It Promotes Stability

Saving helps us avoid financial stress and dependence on others. Proverbs 6:6-8 (AMP) uses the ant as a model of preparation and diligence: "Go to the ant, O lazy one; observe her ways and be wise, which, having no chief, overseer, or ruler, prepares her food in the summer and brings in her provisions [of food for the winter] in the harvest."

3. It Enables Greater Generosity
When we save wisely, we are better equipped to respond to the needs of others.

Generosity: The Key to Unlocking God's Blessings

The Bible consistently teaches that generosity brings blessings, both spiritual and material. Proverbs 11:25 (AMP) states, "The generous man [is a source of blessing and] shall be prosperous and enriched, and he who waters will himself be watered [reaping the generosity he has sown]."

Here are three principles of generosity that align with God's Word:
1. Give Cheerfully
2 Corinthians 9:7 (AMP) says, "Each one should give [thoughtfully and with purpose] just as he has decided in his heart, not grudgingly or under compulsion, for God loves a cheerful giver." Giving is an act of worship and should be done with joy and gratitude.
2. Give Proportionately
Luke 21:1-4 tells the story of the widow who gave all she had. This account reminds us that generosity is not about the amount but the heart behind the gift.
3. Give Expectantly

Generosity positions us to receive God's blessings. Luke 6:38 (AMP) declares, "Give, and it will be given to you. They will pour into your lap a good measure—pressed down, shaken together, and running over [with no space left for more]."

Helping Those in Need: A Biblical Mandate

One of the most direct ways to demonstrate generosity is by helping those in need. The Bible is filled with exhortations to care for the poor, widows, and orphans.

1. God's Heart for the Needy
Psalm 68:5 (AMP) describes God as a "Father of the fatherless and a judge and protector of the widows." Helping the vulnerable reflects His character and fulfills His commands.

2. Practical Ways to Help
- Provide Financial Assistance: Give to trusted charities or directly to individuals in need.
- Offer Time and Skills: Volunteering is a powerful way to serve.
- Advocate for Justice: Speak up for those who cannot speak for themselves (Proverbs 31:8-9).

3. The Rewards of Helping Others
Proverbs 19:17 (AMP) promises, "Whoever is gracious and lends a hand to the poor lends to the Lord, and He will repay him for his good deed." This repayment may come in various forms—peace, joy, spiritual growth, or even material blessings.

Balancing Generosity with Stewardship

While generosity is crucial, it must be balanced with wise stewardship.

Overextending ourselves financially can lead to stress and limit our ability to help in the future. Here are some tips for balancing the two:

1. Set a Giving Budget

Determine a specific percentage of your income for giving, in addition to your tithe.

2. Prioritize Needs

Focus on urgent and essential needs first.

3. Seek God's Guidance

Pray for wisdom in deciding how and where to give. James 1:5 (AMP) says, "If any of you lacks wisdom [to guide him through a decision or circumstance], he is to ask of [our benevolent] God."

The Eternal Impact of Generosity

Generosity extends beyond financial success; it impacts eternity. Matthew 6:19-21 (AMP) advises, "Do not store up for yourselves treasures on earth, where moth and rust destroy, and where thieves break in and steal. But store up for yourselves treasures in heaven... For where your treasure is, there your heart will be also."

When we invest in God's kingdom by helping others, we lay up treasures in heaven. This eternal perspective transforms how we view wealth, shifting our focus from accumulation to contribution.

Conclusion: Prioritizing Money God's Way

By embracing biblical principles—tithing, saving, and generosity—we unlock the secrets to financial success and align our lives with God's will. Helping those in need reflects His heart, brings joy and purpose, and positions us to receive His blessings.

Through faithful stewardship, we honor God, avoid financial stress, and live a life of generosity and peace. In doing so, we fulfill our role as His stewards, leaving a legacy that glorifies Him and impacts lives for generations to come.

Be Honest in Financial Dealings

Managing finances in alignment with God's principles—referred to here as prioritizing money "kingdom style"—is an essential practice for believers who desire to honor God and achieve financial peace. The Bible provides timeless guidance on how to approach wealth, emphasizing values like honesty, generosity, and diligence. Proverbs 13:11 (AMP) states, "Dishonest money dwindles away, but whoever gathers money little by little makes it grow." This verse encapsulates the need for integrity in financial dealings, showing that honest practices build lasting success, while dishonesty leads to loss.

By embracing principles such as tithing, saving, and generosity, Christians can unlock the biblical path to wealth while fulfilling God's purpose in their financial stewardship. This summary explores these key ideas and the crucial role of integrity in financial matters, offering practical guidance for believers who seek faith-based financial wisdom.

Honesty in Financial Dealings: The Foundation of Godly Finances

Integrity is a non-negotiable component of financial stewardship. The Bible repeatedly calls for honesty in all aspects of life, especially in how we handle money.
1. God's Standards for Financial Honesty
Proverbs 16:11 (AMP) declares, "A just balance and [honest] scales are the Lord's; all the weights of the bag are

His concern [established by His eternal principles]." This verse affirms that fairness and honesty in transactions are not just good business practices—they are spiritual responsibilities. Every financial decision we make should align with God's standard of truth.

2. The Consequences of Dishonesty

Dishonesty in financial dealings may bring temporary gain, but it ultimately leads to loss. Proverbs 21:6 (AMP) warns, "Acquiring treasures by a lying tongue is a fleeting vapor [the seeking and pursuit of death]." Deceptive practices not only harm others but also jeopardize our relationship with God and our personal integrity.

3. Integrity as a Testimony

When Christians conduct their financial affairs with integrity, they reflect God's character to the world. Numbers 23:19 (AMP) reminds us, "God is not a man, that He should lie." By being truthful and trustworthy in our financial dealings, we demonstrate God's faithfulness and provide a powerful witness to others.

4. Trust and Security Through Honesty
Proverbs 10:9 (AMP) teaches, "He who walks in integrity and with moral character walks securely." Honesty builds trust, fosters healthy relationships, and creates financial stability. A reputation for integrity opens doors to opportunities and partnerships that dishonesty would destroy.

Tithing: Honoring God First

Tithing is a foundational biblical principle that acknowledges God's sovereignty over our finances. Malachi 3:10 (AMP) commands, "Bring all the tithes (the tenth) into the storehouse... test Me now in this... if I will not open for you the windows of heaven and pour out for you [so great] a blessing."

1. The Spiritual Meaning of Tithing

Tithing is an act of worship, trust, and gratitude. By giving the first 10% of our income to God, we recognize Him as the ultimate provider and owner of all we have.

2. Tithing and Trust

Proverbs 3:9-10 (AMP) states, "Honor the Lord with your wealth and with the first fruits of all your crops; then your barns will be abundantly filled." Tithing teaches us to trust in God's provision, even when resources seem limited.

3. The Blessings of Tithing

Faithful tithing aligns our hearts with God's purposes and invites His blessings. It also positions us to be generous, as God often provides abundantly for those who honor Him with their finances.

4. Tithing as a Form of Integrity
Honesty in tithing means giving to God what is rightfully His. Malachi 3:8 (AMP) warns, "Will a man rob God? Yet you are robbing Me! But you say, 'In what way have we robbed You?' In tithes and offerings [you have withheld]." Faithfulness in tithing is part of living with integrity before God.

Saving: Demonstrating Wisdom and Foresight

The Bible encourages wise planning and saving for the future. Proverbs 21:20 (AMP) explains, "There is precious treasure and oil in the dwelling of the wise [who prepare for the future], but a short-sighted and foolish man swallows it up and wastes it."

1. The Role of Savings in Stewardship
Saving is not about hoarding wealth but about preparing for future needs and opportunities. It reflects foresight, discipline, and a commitment to managing God's resources wisely.

2. Saving Gradually and Honestly
Proverbs 13:11 underscores that wealth gained gradually and honestly is more enduring than wealth acquired through dishonest or hasty means. Consistent saving builds stability and allows for future generosity.

3. Balancing Saving with Generosity
While saving is essential, it must be balanced with a spirit of generosity. Luke 6:38 (AMP) encourages, "Give, and it will be given to you. They will pour into your lap a good measure—pressed down, shaken together, and

running over." Wise saving enables us to give freely without financial strain.

4. Emergency and Long-Term Planning
Saving equips us to handle emergencies, support our families, and invest in opportunities to advance God's kingdom. Ecclesiastes 11:2 (AMP) advises, "Divide your portion among seven, or even eight [investments], for you do not know what misfortune may occur on the earth." Diversifying resources ensures long-term financial stability.

Generosity: Reflecting God's Heart

Generosity is a central theme in kingdom finances, reflecting God's character and His call to care for others. Proverbs 19:17 (AMP) says, "He who is gracious and lends a hand to the poor lends to the Lord, and the Lord will repay him for his good deed."

1. Generosity as Worship

When we give to others, we honor God and acknowledge His provision in our lives. Generosity is a tangible expression of gratitude and faith.

2. The Rewards of Generosity

Scripture promises blessings for those who give freely. Proverbs 11:25 (AMP) states, "The generous man [is a source of blessing and] shall be prosperous and enriched." God often multiplies resources for those who steward them well and share them with others.

3. Generosity and Stewardship

True generosity requires wise financial management. By prioritizing tithing and saving, we ensure that we have the means to bless others without compromising our own financial responsibilities.

4. Generosity Reflects God's Kingdom Values

Helping those in need reflects God's heart for justice and compassion. Isaiah 58:10 (AMP) encourages, "And if you offer yourself to [assist] the hungry and satisfy the need of the afflicted, then your light will rise in darkness." Generosity points others to Christ and advances His kingdom on earth.

Practical Steps to Prioritize Finances God's Way

To align your finances with God's principles, consider these practical steps:

1. Commit Your Finances to God

Begin with prayer, asking God to guide your financial decisions and help you honor Him in all aspects of money management.

2. Create a Budget that Honors God
Develop a budget that includes tithing, saving, and giving. Ensure your spending reflects your values and avoids unnecessary debt.

3. Practice Contentment
Hebrews 13:5 (AMP) reminds us, "Let your character be free from the love of money… being content with what you have." Contentment allows us to focus on eternal priorities rather than worldly possessions.

4. Avoid Debt
Proverbs 22:7 (AMP) warns, "The borrower is servant to the lender." Live within your means and avoid unnecessary debt, which can hinder financial peace and generosity.

5. Invest Wisely

Follow biblical principles of diversification and stewardship when investing resources. Seek counsel and ensure all investments align with your values.

6. Give Cheerfully and Intentionally
2 Corinthians 9:7 (AMP) urges, "Let each one give [thoughtfully and with purpose]... for God loves a cheerful giver." Generosity should be a joyful and purposeful act of worship.

Conclusion: Unlocking the Blessings of Stewardship

Prioritizing money kingdom style involves more than managing a budget—it's about honoring God, trusting His provision, and living out His principles in every financial decision. By practicing honesty, tithing faithfully, saving wisely, and giving generously, we align ourselves with God's will and invite His blessings into our lives.

Proverbs 13:11 reminds us that wealth gained honestly and gradually leads to lasting success. As we embrace these principles, we not only achieve financial peace but also reflect God's kingdom values, advancing His purposes on earth and glorifying His name.

Don't Place Trust in Wealth

The Bible offers timeless wisdom for managing money in a way that honors God and leads to lasting peace and fulfillment. One of the central themes in Scripture is the call to place our trust in God rather than in wealth. As 1 Timothy 6:17 (AMP) warns, "Command those who are rich in this present world not to be arrogant nor to put their hope in wealth, which is so uncertain, but to put their hope in God, who richly and ceaselessly provides us with everything for our enjoyment." This principle reminds believers that wealth is fleeting, but a life rooted in faith brings eternal security.

By focusing on key biblical principles like tithing, saving, and generosity, this summary explores how to prioritize money in a way that aligns with God's kingdom. Trusting in God rather than wealth is at the heart of financial stewardship, offering a pathway to true success and peace.

The Danger of Trusting in Wealth

Wealth can easily become an idol, drawing our focus away from God. The Bible provides numerous warnings against placing our security in material possessions.
1. The Uncertainty of Riches
Wealth, while useful, is unreliable. Proverbs 23:4-5 (AMP) states, "Do not weary yourself [with the overwhelming desire] to gain wealth; cease from your own understanding of it. When you set your eyes on it, it is gone. For wealth certainly makes itself wings like an

eagle that flies to the heavens." This vivid imagery illustrates how quickly riches can disappear, making it foolish to depend on them for security.

2. The Deception of Wealth

Jesus cautioned His followers about the deceitfulness of riches in Matthew 13:22 (AMP): "The deceitfulness of [superficial] pleasures and delight of riches choke the word, and it yields no fruit." Trusting in wealth can blind us to spiritual truths, leading to a life of emptiness despite material abundance.

3. Arrogance Rooted in Wealth

Wealth can breed pride and self-sufficiency. 1 Timothy 6:17 commands believers not to become arrogant because of their riches. Pride distances us from God and others, making it harder to live a life of humility and service.

4. Eternal Perspective on Wealth
Jesus reminds us in Matthew 6:19-21 (AMP): "Do not store up for yourselves treasures on earth, where moth and rust destroy, and where thieves break in and steal. But store up for yourselves treasures in heaven... For where your treasure is, there your heart will be also." True security comes from investing in eternal riches, such as faith, love, and acts of generosity.

Placing Trust in God

Trusting in God rather than wealth is a fundamental aspect of kingdom living. It shifts our focus from temporary resources to the eternal source of provision.
1. God's Faithful Provision
Matthew 6:31-33 (AMP) assures believers, "Do not worry or be

anxious... for your heavenly Father knows that you need them. But first and most importantly seek His kingdom and His righteousness... and all these things will be given to you also." Trusting God's provision brings peace and eliminates the anxiety that often accompanies financial concerns.

2. Hope Beyond Wealth

Wealth is temporary, but God's promises are eternal. Psalm 62:10 (AMP) advises, "If riches increase, do not set your heart on them." Instead, believers are encouraged to place their hope in God, who provides lasting joy and fulfillment.

3. Faith Over Fear

Trusting in God frees us from the fear of financial insecurity. Philippians 4:19 (AMP) promises, "My God will liberally supply [fill until full] your every need according to His riches in glory in Christ

Jesus." This assurance allows believers to approach finances with confidence, knowing that God is in control.

4. Spiritual Riches Over Material Wealth

Revelation 3:17-18 (AMP) highlights the emptiness of material riches compared to spiritual wealth: "You say, 'I am rich, and have prospered and grown wealthy, and have need of nothing,' but you do not know that you are wretched and miserable and poor and blind and naked [without hope and in great need]." True wealth comes from a relationship with Christ, not from material possessions.

Tithing: Honoring God First

Tithing is a tangible way to place our trust in God and prioritize Him over wealth. By giving the first portion of our income to God, we acknowledge His sovereignty and demonstrate faith in His provision.

1. Biblical Command for Tithing

Malachi 3:10 (AMP) declares, "Bring all the tithes (the tenth) into the storehouse… test Me now in this… if I will not open for you the windows of heaven." Tithing not only fulfills a biblical command but also invites God's blessings into our lives.

2. Trust Through Tithing

Proverbs 3:9-10 (AMP) states, "Honor the Lord with your wealth and with the first fruits of all your crops; then your barns will be abundantly filled." Giving to God first demonstrates trust in His ability to meet our needs, even when resources seem scarce.

3. Tithing as a Heart Check

Tithing reveals our priorities. Matthew 6:21 (AMP) reminds us, "Where your treasure is, there your heart will be also." By giving generously to God, we show that our hearts are set on His kingdom rather than earthly wealth.

4. The Joy of Generosity

2 Corinthians 9:7 (AMP) encourages cheerful giving: "God loves a cheerful giver [and delights in the one whose heart is in his gift]." Tithing becomes a source of joy when we view it as an act of worship and trust.

Saving: Exercising Wisdom and Discipline

While tithing focuses on giving, saving emphasizes stewardship and preparation for the future. Both are essential components of kingdom finances.

1. Biblical Examples of Saving

Proverbs 21:20 (AMP) explains, "There is precious treasure and oil in the dwelling of the wise [who prepare for the future], but a short-sighted and foolish man swallows it up and wastes it." Saving is an act of wisdom that ensures resources are available for future needs.

2. Avoiding the Trap of Hoarding
While saving is important, it must not become an idol. Luke 12:15 (AMP) warns, "Be on guard against every form of greed... not even when one has an overflowing abundance does his life consist of [nor is it derived from] his possessions." Saving should be balanced with generosity and trust in God.

3. The Role of Discipline in Saving
Consistent saving requires discipline and self-control. Proverbs 13:11 (AMP) advises, "Wealth [not earned but] won

in haste or unjustly... will dwindle, but he who gathers gradually by honest labor will increase [his riches]." Small, consistent efforts lead to lasting financial stability.

4. Saving and Faith

Saving does not contradict faith in God's provision. Instead, it reflects responsible stewardship and foresight, enabling believers to meet future needs and support others.

Generosity: Reflecting God's Heart

Generosity is a hallmark of kingdom finances, reflecting God's character and advancing His purposes.

1. Biblical Command for Generosity

Proverbs 19:17 (AMP) states, "He who is gracious and lends a hand to the poor lends to the Lord, and the Lord will repay him for his good deed."

Generosity is both a privilege and a responsibility for believers.

2. The Joy of Giving

Acts 20:35 (AMP) reminds us, "It is more blessed [and brings greater joy] to give than to receive." Giving brings joy, not only to the recipient but also to the giver, as it aligns with God's generous nature.

3. Generosity as Worship

Giving to others is an act of worship that honors God. Hebrews 13:16 (AMP) encourages believers, "Do not neglect to do good, to contribute [to the needy of the church as an expression of fellowship], for such sacrifices are always pleasing to God."

4. Trusting God Through Generosity

Generosity requires faith, as it involves releasing resources without fear of lack. Luke 6:38 (AMP) promises, "Give, and it will be given to you. They will pour into your lap a good measure—pressed down, shaken together, and running over." God honors those who give freely and generously.

Practical Steps to Prioritize Finances God's Way

To align finances with God's principles, consider these practical steps:
1. Surrender Finances to God
Begin with prayer, committing your finances to God and asking for His wisdom and guidance.
2. Tithe Faithfully
Prioritize tithing as an act of worship and trust, giving the first portion of your income to God.
3. Save Strategically
Develop a savings plan that balances preparation for the future with a reliance on God's provision.

4. Give Generously
Look for opportunities to bless others, whether through charitable giving, supporting ministries, or helping those in need.

5. Avoid Debt
Live within your means and avoid unnecessary debt, which can hinder financial freedom and generosity.

6. Seek Contentment
Embrace contentment by focusing on God's provision rather than material possessions.

7. Invest in Eternal Treasures
Prioritize spending and giving that advances God's kingdom, recognizing that true wealth lies in eternal rewards.

Conclusion: Trusting God for True Financial Success

Unlocking biblical secrets to financial success begins with placing our trust in God rather than wealth. By practicing tithing, saving, and generosity, believers can honor God, avoid financial stress, and live a life of peace and purpose.

1 Timothy 6:17 reminds us that wealth is temporary, but God's provision is eternal. By following His principles and prioritizing finances kingdom style, we can experience true success—rooted not in material possessions but in a deep, abiding relationship with Christ.

Budget Wisely

The Bible provides clear guidance on how to manage finances in a way that honors God and promotes peace, generosity, and security. Central to this is the principle of budgeting wisely. Luke 14:28 (AMP) says, "Suppose one of you wants to build a tower. Will he not first sit down and calculate the cost to see if he has enough to finish it?" This verse underscores the necessity of planning and budgeting as a foundational part of financial stewardship. By following a biblically aligned approach to budgeting, believers can prioritize their finances in a way that reflects kingdom values.

Effective financial stewardship involves careful planning, disciplined saving, consistent tithing, and joyful generosity. These principles, combined with a reliance on God's provision, lead to both financial stability and spiritual growth. Below, we explore how budgeting wisely aligns with God's Word and serves as a pathway to unlocking biblical secrets to financial success.

The Biblical Case for Budgeting
1. Planning as a Biblical Principle
Budgeting is essentially a form of planning, which the Bible encourages repeatedly. Proverbs 21:5 (AMP) states, "The plans of the diligent lead surely to abundance and advantage, but everyone who acts in haste comes surely to poverty." Creating a budget helps believers steward their resources wisely and avoid impulsive decisions that lead to financial stress.
2. Counting the Cost

Luke 14:28 highlights the importance of assessing resources before undertaking any project. A budget ensures that financial commitments are realistic and aligned with available resources. This prevents overspending and creates a foundation for wise decision-making.

3. Avoiding Wastefulness

Proverbs 27:23-24 (AMP) advises, "Know well the condition of your flocks, and pay attention to your herds; for riches are not forever." This verse illustrates the need to monitor resources closely and allocate them responsibly. A budget is a practical tool for doing this, ensuring that income is used effectively and not squandered.

Why Budgeting Honors God

1. Demonstrates Stewardship

Psalm 24:1 (AMP) reminds us, "The earth is the Lord's, and everything in it." As stewards of God's resources, believers are called to manage finances responsibly. Budgeting is an act of stewardship, acknowledging that all resources ultimately belong to God.

2. Promotes Generosity

A well-planned budget creates margin for generosity. Ephesians 4:28 (AMP) says, "...so that he will have something to share with those in need." By budgeting, believers can ensure they have the means to give freely and support others.

3. Reflects Trust in God

Budgeting is not a sign of mistrust but a way to align financial practices with God's provision. Proverbs 3:5-6 (AMP) encourages us, "Trust in and rely confidently on the Lord with all your heart… and He will make your paths straight and smooth." Budgeting with prayerful dependence on God demonstrates faith in His guidance.

Practical Steps to Budget Wisely
1. Set Financial Goals
Begin by identifying short-term and long-term financial goals. These should align with biblical values, such as tithing, saving, and giving. Proverbs 16:3 (AMP) advises, "Commit your works to the Lord [submit and trust them to Him], and your plans will succeed [if you respond to His will and guidance]."
2. Track Income and Expenses
Understanding where your money is coming from and where it is going is essential for creating an effective budget. Proverbs 27:23 emphasizes the importance of being aware of your resources.

3. Prioritize Needs Over Wants

A kingdom-focused budget prioritizes essentials, such as housing, food, and healthcare, while avoiding unnecessary spending. Philippians 4:19 (AMP) assures us, "My God will liberally supply [fill until full] your every need according to His riches in glory in Christ Jesus." This promise encourages contentment and trust in God for our needs.

4. Allocate for Tithing and Giving

The first portion of any budget should go to God. Malachi 3:10 (AMP) says, "Bring all the tithes (the tenth) into the storehouse... if I will not open for you the windows of heaven and pour out for you [so great] a blessing." Giving to God first honors Him and invites His blessings.

5. Create a Savings Plan

Saving is a biblical principle that reflects wisdom and preparation. Proverbs 21:20 (AMP) states, "There is precious treasure and oil in the dwelling of the wise [who prepare for the future]." A portion of your income should be set aside for emergencies and future needs.

6. Reduce Debt

Debt can hinder financial freedom and generosity. Proverbs 22:7 (AMP) warns, "The borrower is servant to the lender." A budget should include a plan to pay off debts systematically while avoiding new ones.

7. Review and Adjust Regularly

A budget is a living document that should be reviewed regularly to ensure it remains effective. Changes in income or expenses may require adjustments, and regular reviews keep spending aligned with goals and priorities.

Budgeting for Generosity

1. The Joy of Giving

Acts 20:35 (AMP) reminds us, "It is more blessed and brings greater joy to give than to receive." Budgeting for generosity ensures that giving is intentional and consistent.

2. Supporting Kingdom Work

A well-planned budget enables believers to support ministries, missions, and charitable organizations. 2 Corinthians 9:6-7 (AMP) says, "Now [remember] this: he who sows sparingly will also reap sparingly… for God loves a cheerful giver [and delights in the one whose heart is in his gift]."

3. Helping Those in Need

Proverbs 19:17 (AMP) states, "He who is gracious and lends a hand to the poor lends to the Lord, and the Lord will repay him for his good deed." Budgeting for generosity allows believers to respond to the needs of others with compassion and love.

Avoiding Common Pitfalls
1. Neglecting to Plan
Failing to budget often leads to overspending and financial stress. Proverbs 29:18 (AMP) warns, "Where there is no vision [no revelation of God and His word], the people are unrestrained." A budget provides the vision needed for disciplined financial management.
2. Overlooking God's Guidance
James 1:5 (AMP) encourages believers to seek wisdom: "If any of you lacks wisdom, let him ask of God... and it will be given to him." Prayerfully seeking God's guidance ensures that budgeting decisions align with His will.

3. Ignoring Emergencies
A lack of savings can lead to panic during unexpected events. Proverbs 6:6-8 (AMP) praises the ant for storing provisions during the summer. Planning for emergencies is an act of wisdom that reflects biblical principles.

4. Focusing Solely on Wealth
A budget that prioritizes material wealth over spiritual growth misses the heart of kingdom living. Matthew 6:33 (AMP) reminds us, "But first and most importantly seek (aim at, strive after) His kingdom and His righteousness." Finances should serve God's purposes, not the other way around.

The Spiritual Benefits of Budgeting
1. Peace of Mind
A well-planned budget reduces financial anxiety, allowing believers to

focus on their relationship with God. Philippians 4:6-7 (AMP) encourages us, "Do not be anxious or worried about anything... and the peace of God [that peace which reassures the heart] will stand guard over your hearts and minds in Christ Jesus."

2. Freedom to Serve

Financial stability creates the freedom to serve others and participate in kingdom work. Romans 12:13 (AMP) urges believers, "Contribute to the needs of God's people [sharing in the necessities of the saints]."

3. Testimony to Others

Responsible budgeting and financial stewardship serve as a testimony to God's faithfulness. Matthew 5:16 (AMP) says, "Let your light shine before men in such a way that they may see your good deeds and moral excellence, and [recognize and honor and] glorify your Father who is in heaven."

Conclusion: Budgeting Wisely to Honor God

Budgeting is a powerful tool for aligning finances with God's kingdom principles. It reflects responsible stewardship, fosters generosity, and ensures that resources are used in ways that glorify God. By creating a budget that prioritizes tithing, saving, and giving, believers can avoid financial stress, live generously, and experience the peace that comes from trusting in God's provision.

As Luke 14:28 reminds us, budgeting is not just a practical necessity but a biblical mandate. By counting the cost and planning wisely, believers can unlock the secrets to financial success while honoring God in every aspect of their lives. Through prayerful planning and faithful stewardship, we can live out the biblical path to wealth, experiencing the joy and fulfillment that comes from trusting God and using His resources for His glory.

Invest Wisely

The Bible offers profound wisdom on managing money, emphasizing principles that lead to both spiritual and financial growth. Among these principles is the call to invest wisely. Ecclesiastes 11:6 (AMP) states, "Sow your seed in the morning, and at evening do not withhold your hand, for you do not know which activity will prosper—whether this one or that, or whether both alike will be good." This scripture encourages diversification and diligence, highlighting the importance of spreading resources across various opportunities for greater chances of success.

To prioritize finances kingdom-style, believers must align their financial habits with biblical principles, focusing on stewardship, faith, and practical wisdom. Wise investment is a critical component of this, allowing individuals to grow their resources, support kingdom work, and provide for their families and communities. Below, we delve into the biblical foundations for wise investing and explore how this principle integrates with tithes, savings, and generosity for holistic financial stewardship.

The Biblical Foundation for Investing
1. Investment Reflects God's Design for Stewardship
The concept of investing aligns with the biblical principle of stewardship. Matthew 25:14-30 (AMP) illustrates this in the Parable of the Talents, where servants were entrusted with their master's resources. The ones who invested and multiplied their talents

were commended, while the servant who buried his was rebuked. This parable underscores the importance of using resources wisely to generate growth.

2. Faith and Diligence in the Unknown
Ecclesiastes 11:6 emphasizes faith and diligence in sowing seed, even when outcomes are uncertain. Investing requires a balance of trust in God and proactive effort. By diversifying resources and seeking multiple opportunities, believers can participate in God's provision and the growth He enables.

3. Preparation for the Future
Proverbs 6:6-8 (AMP) praises the ant for storing provisions in the summer, demonstrating foresight and preparation. Investing is a practical way to prepare for future needs,

aligning with the biblical call to plan and act wisely.

Why Wise Investing Honors God
1. Faithfulness in Managing Resources
Luke 16:10-11 (AMP) states, "Whoever is faithful in a very little thing is also faithful in much... If you have not been faithful in the use of earthly wealth, who will entrust the true riches to you?" Investing wisely demonstrates faithfulness in handling the resources God has entrusted to us, ensuring they are used for His purposes.
2. Multiplying Resources for Kingdom Work
Wise investments generate returns that can be used to advance God's kingdom. Acts 4:34-35 (AMP) describes early Christians who shared their resources generously, ensuring no one was in need. Through investment,

believers can grow their wealth to support ministries, missions, and those in need.

3. Reflecting God's Creativity and Wisdom

Genesis 1:28 (AMP) calls humanity to "fill the earth and subdue it [putting it under your power]." Investing reflects this mandate by utilizing creativity, wisdom, and effort to cultivate and grow what God has provided.

Practical Steps to Invest Wisely

1. Seek God's Guidance

Before making investment decisions, seek God's wisdom through prayer and His Word. James 1:5 (AMP) promises, "If any of you lacks wisdom, let him ask of God... and it will be given to him."

2. Diversify Your Investments

Ecclesiastes 11:2 (AMP) advises, "Divide your portion to seven, or even to eight, for you do not know what misfortune may occur on the earth." Diversification reduces risk by spreading resources across different opportunities. This applies to financial investments, businesses, and even charitable endeavors.

3. Invest with Integrity

Proverbs 13:11 (AMP) warns, "Wealth obtained by fraud dwindles, but he who gathers gradually by honest labor will increase [his riches]." Ethical investing ensures that financial growth aligns with kingdom values. Avoid investments tied to unethical practices, focusing instead on opportunities that reflect God's righteousness.

4. Consider Long-Term Growth

Proverbs 21:5 (AMP) states, "The plans of the diligent lead surely to abundance and advantage." Investing requires patience and a focus on long-term gains rather than short-term profits. Strategic planning and diligence are key.

5. Educate Yourself

Proverbs 4:7 (AMP) emphasizes the value of wisdom: "The beginning of wisdom is: Get [skillful and godly] wisdom [it is preeminent]! And with all your acquiring, get understanding [actively seek spiritual discernment]." Understanding investment options, risks, and strategies is essential for making informed decisions.

6. Start Small but Stay Consistent

Luke 16:10 teaches that faithfulness in small things leads to greater opportunities. Begin with manageable investments and remain consistent, trusting God to multiply your efforts over time.

How Investing Complements Other Financial Principles

1. Tithes and Investments

Tithing remains a foundational principle in biblical finances. Malachi 3:10 (AMP) says, "Bring all the tithes (the tenth) into the storehouse... and see if I will not open for you the windows of heaven." While investing grows resources, tithing honors God as the ultimate provider. A balanced financial plan incorporates both.

2. Savings and Investments

Proverbs 21:20 (AMP) highlights the wisdom of saving: "There is precious treasure and oil in the dwelling of the wise [who prepare for the future]." Saving and investing work together, with savings providing a safety net and investments generating growth.

3. Generosity and Investments

Proverbs 11:25 (AMP) states, "The generous man [is a source of blessing and] shall be prosperous and enriched." Returns from investments enable greater generosity, allowing believers to bless others while glorifying God.

Avoiding Common Pitfalls in Investing
1. Greed and Impatience
1 Timothy 6:9-10 (AMP) warns, "For the love of money is a root of all sorts of evil." Avoid greed-driven decisions and focus on investments that align with God's purposes.
2. Neglecting Stewardship Principles
Investing should never overshadow biblical principles of stewardship, such as tithing, generosity, and avoiding debt. Maintain a balanced approach that prioritizes obedience to God over financial gain.

3. Risk Without Discernment
Proverbs 22:3 (AMP) says, "A prudent and farsighted person sees the evil and hides himself." Avoid risky investments that could lead to significant losses. Research thoroughly and seek godly counsel before making decisions.
4. Placing Trust in Wealth
1 Timothy 6:17 (AMP) cautions, "Do not put your hope in uncertain riches, but on God." Investments are tools for growth, not sources of ultimate security. Trust in God, not in financial returns.

The Spiritual Benefits of Wise Investing
1. Enables Greater Kingdom Impact
Investing grows resources that can be used to support missions, ministries, and charitable work. Matthew 6:20 (AMP) encourages believers to "store up for yourselves treasures in heaven."

Wise investing allows for eternal impact.

2. Promotes Peace of Mind

Proverbs 3:5-6 (AMP) reminds us to trust in God's guidance. Wise investing, coupled with faith, provides financial stability and peace, freeing believers from anxiety about the future.

3. Fosters Growth in Faith

Investing requires trust in God for results, as Ecclesiastes 11:6 suggests. This dependence on God deepens faith and reinforces His role as the ultimate provider.

Practical Example: Applying Biblical Investing

Consider a believer who receives a salary and desires to honor God with their finances. They tithe faithfully, set aside savings, and invest a portion of their income in opportunities that align with kingdom values. They diversify their investments, prayerfully seek God's guidance, and remain patient, trusting Him for growth. Over time, their investments yield returns, enabling them to give generously, support missions, and create a legacy of faithfulness for future generations.

Conclusion: Investing Wisely for God's Glory

Investing wisely is a key component of kingdom-style financial management, reflecting diligence, stewardship, and trust in God. Ecclesiastes 11:6 reminds us to sow diligently, trusting God to bring the increase. By diversifying resources, planning carefully, and aligning investments with biblical values, believers can achieve financial growth while honoring God.

When combined with principles of tithing, saving, and generosity, investing becomes a powerful tool for advancing God's kingdom and living out His purposes. By following the biblical path to wealth, we can unlock the secrets to financial success, experience peace, and create lasting impact for God's glory.

About Scott Perdue

Scott Perdue is a dynamic entrepreneur, author, and community leader with a life rooted in faith, family, and service. A devoted Christian, Scott has been married for over 20 years and is the proud father of four children—two girls and two boys. His passion for personal development and spiritual growth is reflected in his prolific writing career, having authored over 80 books, most of which focus on self-help and Christian themes. His books have touched the lives of countless readers seeking guidance on how to lead a fulfilling, faith-centered life.

For over 15 years, Scott has been a dedicated member of GUTS Church, a place he fondly refers to as "It Takes GUTS to Serve the Lord." His service to the church and community extends beyond attendance; he spent six years as a representative for the GUTS Food Bank, where he managed the movement of wholesale goods to help those in need. Scott also led a successful Maximized Manhood study group based on Edwin Cole's teachings, further exemplifying his commitment to fostering spiritual growth among men.

An accomplished entrepreneur, Scott has started and operated over 30 businesses, ranging from pest control to contracting. He is the founder of Universal Bug Man, a pest control service where Scott earned a reputation as a "pest control superhero." His entrepreneurial ventures include Tulsa Furniture Wholesale, Tulsa Auction Spot, and Builderhaus Unlimited, among others. Scott's business acumen extends to the health and wellness industry, where his company HCG Medical helped over 20,000 clients lose weight, generating over $6.5 million in sales in its best year.

Scott Perdue is a man of many talents, driven by his faith and dedication to serving others through his varied enterprises and writing.

Scott Perdue Books (on Amazon)

Christian Books by Scott Perdue:

Biblical Entrepreneur Leadership: Amplified Leverage Business Skills Book & Workbook

Biblical Men's Leadership Skills: Becoming an Amplified Christian Superstar Book & Workbook

Unleashing Biblical Manhood: Taking Ground Like a Warrior Book & Workbook

Promised Land Leadership: Leading an Army Like Joshua

Wilderness Wisdom of Moses: Timeless Life-Changing Leadership Lessons

Rules of Christianity According to Paul Book & Workbook

Provisional Miracles of Jesus: Provision through Supernatural Means Book & Workbook

The King's Highway: Lean into Jesus for Accelerated Success

Walk in the Works of the Lord: An Amplified Passion Understanding

God's River: Getting into the Kingdom Family Flow

Forgiven & Unoffendable: The Power of Walking Righteously

God is Real: Knowing the Spirit - A Journey Through Faith, Miracles, and Divine Presence

Living on Purpose: A Comprehensive Guide to a Meaningful and Fulfilling Life

Praying for Others: Unlocking your God-Given Authority to Change Lives

Speaking in Tongues: Snippets of Life Improvement Code

Be Fruitful and Multiply: A Biblical Guide to Family Planning and Takes

Biblical Map of the Garden of Eden: Where does this Mysterious Garden Exist?

Methuselah: The Biblical Legacy of Noah's Grandfather

Love's Crossroads: The Rewards of Suffering for Love

Features of a Great Christian Camp: A Priority Spiritual Foundation

Daily Mercy: A Journey Through God's Grace Every Morning

Self Help Books by Scott Perdue:

You Are the Masterpiece: Center of the Universe Life Experience

Legacy Blueprint: How to Build a Generational Legacy

Accomplishing Greatness: 10 Legendary Skill Sets of Self-Made Millionaires

Beginners Guide to Investing in the Future: Gain Wealth from Cutting Edge Sectors

Motivation for Creation: Unlocking the Spark Within

10 Step Productivity Plan: A Guide to Increasing Life's Results

Mindset of Productivity: A Defined Focused Journey

Mindful Love: Embracing Self Love Through Mindfulness and Compassion

The Ultimate Guide to Winning Friends and Influencing People: Master Communication

The Human Connection: Unlocking the Secrets to Understanding and Relating to Others

Mind Switch: Are you Over-Thinking Negative Thoughts?

Mastering Self-Control: Unleashing the Power of Discipline for Success in Every Aspect of Life

Unlocking Secrets to Weight Loss: A Comprehensive Guide to Science, Nutrition, and Wellness

Effective Diet Supplements for Weight Loss

The Body Detox Blueprint: 10 Essential Steps to Cleanse, Heal, and Revitalize Your Body

Secret 1000 Calorie Cryogenic Diet

Learn to Enjoy Reading: Your Ultimate Guide to Loving Books

The Ultimate Blueprint to Comedy: Your Guide to Mastering Humor and Making People Laugh

Decluttering Your Home: Take Control of Your Space, One Step at a Time

Real Estate Needs Observation: Hot to Bring Light to Entropy & Chaos

Business Books by Scott Perdue:

Legendary Business Skills: How to Think like an Entrepreneur

Seal the Deal: Mastering Sales Objections to Close Every Sale

10 Step Marketing Launch: Ultimate Guide for a Business Advertising Start Up

Email Marketing Success: 10 Ways to Master Business Email Advertising Strategy

Controlled Decent: How to Close a Business

How to Start a Business Networking Group: Learn to Organize and Motivate Business Leaders

Negotiate Like an Auctioneer: Mastering the Art of Persuasion and Control

Auction House Blueprint: How to Win Bids and Host a Successful Auction

How to Run an Antique Shop: Restoring Antique Relics to Modern Living

Secondhand Success: A Complete Guide to Running a Profitable Used Furniture Store

The Thrift Store Playbook: How to Build, Manage, and Thrive in the Resale Business

How to Start an RV Park: Your Roadmap to Success

Turn Rapids to Revenue: How to Run a Profitable River Float Business

Science Books by Scott Perdue:

Creation of Your Galactic Record: Big Bang, DNA, Zodiac, Creation of the Universe. Boom!

Quantum Cosmos: The Wave Function of the Universe

An Astronauts Heavenly Perspective: Planet, Society and Economy

Earth is the Seed of Life: A Geometric Flower of Life

Infinite Plants in Every Seed

Dodecahedron Earth: Exploring the Geometric Key to the Flower of Life

Pangaea Cracked Open: A Pre-Flood World without Oceans

Ancient Cathedral Architecture: A Language Of Semantics Lost in Time

Power Independence: DIY Guide to Building Off-Grid Energy Systems

Harvesting Heaven: The Ultimate Guide to DIY Rainwater Collection Systems

Farming Tactics for the Sahara Desert: Ultimate Gardening Guide for Arid Takes

Easy to Find Herbal Remedies

How to Build Free Energy Lighting: 10 Effective Easy to Build Free Energy Lights

Dynamic Forces: Exploring the Undeniable Power of Movement

Creative Books by Scott Perdue:

Zeppelin Airship Enterprise: The Future of Flight and Travel Reimagined

Ancient Plasma Energy Weapons Revealed: The Lost Technology of Energy Weapons

Echoes of Camelot: Unveiling the Secrets and Legends of the Knights

Secret Treasures of Rome Revealed: Explore the Ancient Architecture of Rome

Giants, Nephilim, and the Legacy of Humanity: From Ancient Myths to Modern Mysteries

Prophecy of the Seven Suns: Exploring Parhelia in Biblical Prophecy

Epic Scavenger Hunt of Machu Picchu

Adventures of Buying an Island: Edge of Your Seat Suspense Thriller Adventure

My Neighbor is an Inventor: A Journey into Wilson's World of Innovation

Adventures of the Zoo Janitor: Growing Responsibility By Excellence

Exile's Genesis: Chronicles of the New Frontier

Relics of Oklahoma: Route 66 Treasure Hunt

The Oklahoma Waterfall Hunt

www.ingramcontent.com/pod-product-compliance
Lightning Source LLC
Chambersburg PA
CBHW071043240526
45471CB00014B/438